Sous Vide Cookbook for Beginners

Easy-to-Follow Guide to
Cooking Restaurant-Quality Meals at Home

Christopher Lester

Table of Contents

Introduction

Magic pots, tablecloths, and wishing tables that can deck themselves with foods are mentioned in legends and tales all over the world. Frankly speaking, I also used to dream of one, especially when I had to come up with some dinner after a long day of work. Well, **with modern cooking appliances, the fairy tales have gotten closer than ever to being real.**

The grains and bakery had long been delegated to the multicooker and bread-making machine; however, that wasn't too much help in a house full of **meat-eaters and fish-lovers**. And, let's admit it, the main course is one of the most difficult things to cook. One extra minute and a **juicy piece of meat** can turn into a dry piece of tasteless fibers. On the other hand, if you take it off the fire too early, it might stay raw. Moreover, even a perfectly cooked meal will lose much of its flavor if frozen, or even when simply left overnight in the fridge. Of course, everyone would prefer some **freshly made, juicy and crispy main meal for dinner**, but how tiresome it is to stand by the cooker with a kitchen thermometer in one hand and a spatula in the other, afraid to take your eyes off the frying pan for a mere second.

Have you ever wondered how they manage to do those **super tender mega-tasty meats in restaurants and cafes**? Actually, it's not a secret anymore—most of them own a truly magic device with a French name, *Sous Vide* (pronounced "soo veed"). The foods in it are cooked at lower temperatures (usually about 130-140 °F). This way, no part of the product is ever heated above its ideal cooking temperature, which ensures even cooking while **saving all the juiciness and tenderness.**

And the other good news is that recently there have appeared quite a few **Sous Vide machines** that can be perfectly used at home. You read that, right! This promising solution for the trickiest meals can now serve you, even in your home kitchen!

Can it get any better than that? Actually, it can… with the book you are holding now! We've collected all the most relevant tips and the best recipes to make sure that your **Sous Vide experience is truly perfect.**

By the way, Sous Vide makes not only an excellent match for **meat and fish**, but is ideally suited to make the most delicious **vegetables, side dishes, fruit, and desserts**. Get familiar with the tips and advice, and then select a recipe that catches your eye. As you get more experienced, you can start experimenting with the settings and products, or just keep following instructions for your favorite dishes.

What is Sous Vide?

The name itself can be translated as "under vacuum".

- Food cooked Sous Vide is usually placed in an **airtight container**.

- This container can then be filled with a **sauce or marinade**.

- After you've added **herbs and spices**, the container is vacuum-sealed and put in a large pot of water.

- The main idea behind this method is that water shall **never heat up** above the desired temperature of doneness.

- The products never get in touch with the metal surface of your pan, and **never get burned or overheated**, providing for a very well-controlled, gradual cooking process at low temperatures.

One thing to keep in mind is that this way of cooking is rather time-consuming. Cooking chicken strips or shrimp will take about an hour, and meals that are more complex require about 6-8 hours on average. Some meals can be cooked for up to 48 hours. However, **you won't have to be around all that time.** You can just set the time and temperature, and you are free until the end of the cooking process.

How Has Sous Vide Emerged?

Basically, Sous Vide is a combination of three cooking approaches: **sealed cooking**—where the food doesn't have any immediate contact with the cooking media, the use of **low temperatures**, and the use of **vacuum.** Therefore, let's look at the history of the three.

The first known sealed-cooking practices date as far back as the Middle Ages, when people came up with an idea of cooking food within animal bladders and intestines. A lot of traditional dishes, particularly in Scotch and Russian cuisine, are still made this way.

The idea of **cooking at low temperatures is also quite old**, and some say that it emerged from various sun-dried foods. But the first attempt to artificially create a medium for low-temperature cooking was recorded in 1799 when American-born British physicist and inventor Benjamin Thompson used the machine he had invented to dry potatoes and to roast meat in it. It was evenly cooked and well done, but the process was costly and time-consuming.

The last aspect of Sous Vide's success is much younger. **Cooking under pressure** was developed by a group of American and French engineers only in the 1960s as one of the industrial food preservation methods. The customers soon said that pressure this pressure method not only prolonged the useful life of products but also improved their flavor and texture.

In the 1970s, a French chef, Georges Pralus, tried using pressure to cook *foie gras* (duck or goose liver) and was very happy with the results—the dish kept its appearance, but had a far better texture and didn't lose fat during the cooking process. At the same time, another Frenchman named Bruno Goussault was **experimenting with low temperatures**. As the chief scientist for a major food manufacturer, he had developed the optimal parameters of cooking times for different foods and temperatures.

Eventually, the two men began collaborating and combined vacuum sealing with low-temperature cooking, thus creating what we now know as *Sous Vide*.

What Equipment will One Need to Cook Sous Vide?

The main idea of a Sous Vide machine is warming water to a constant temperature and moving it around to keep the temperature even all over the surface.

Restaurants and cafés are using extremely expensive large cookers to prepare large quantities of food. On the other hand, culinary consultant Kenji López-Alt suggests using a beer cooler filled with warm water and zip-lock bags for your first Sous Vide experience, but he acknowledges that this might work only for the simplest recipes with a cooking time of about an hour.

So, following is the equipment that you can get for a decent price to enjoy high-quality Sous Vide cooking at your home:

Immersion Circulator or Sous Vide Cooker:

The circulator is a **special wand-style device that you can put inside any usual pot**. It will draw water from the pot, heat it up to the set temperature, and spit it back, thus providing for both circulation and warming of the water.

Another option may be Sous Vide Cooker: **a special pan or a tub with a heated metal coil to warm water to a constant temperature,** making sure that it never fluctuates to a high or low extreme. Such tubs are rather easy to use, but not very compact, and they also restrict you to the use of the same size container.

Cambro Containers:

Pots are fine, but if you want to cook big, consider purchasing some **Cambro containers**. This way, you will get better insulation than with the pot, and at the same time, will be able to choose the size container that meets your needs for the day. Is it a 3-person meal in a small Cambro, or a whole bunch of steaks to be ready for the party tonight? It's up to you!

Food-grade plastic bags and sealer or sealed bags:

Sealed food-grade plastic bags will be necessary, as that's where you put the ingredients. The ideal and most professional option, though, of course, is to use a **vacuum sealer**.

However, you can also opt for zipper-lock freezer bags. Having said this, please, do not try anything thinner than that, because the seal on thinner bags (ones without a lock) is highly likely to degrade and break when you are cooking.

How and What You Can Cook Sous Vide?

Actually, Sous Vide can be used to cook anything that doesn't require water to be heated above the steam point. In other words, you cannot cook pastries, baked goods, pasta, and some cereals. If it's anything else—meat, fish, seafood of any size and texture, vegetables, fruit, desserts, side dishes —

all can be perfectly made with Sous Vide. These are some simple steps that will take you to the world of delicious Sous Vide foods:

Step 1: Select the Recipe

You can select any of the recipes from the book, or try cooking a meal of your own. Many experts say that the best first meal is steak; it's easy to cook and ideally illustrates the advantages of Sous Vide.

Step 2: Cut the Ingredients (if necessary)

If you need to cut or slice the ingredients, make sure that they are cut evenly. So, for example, all meat slices should be of about the same thickness.

Step 3: Season the Ingredients

If you are using some brine, sauce, herbs, or spices, make sure to rub them into the ingredients. Whether it is black pepper, chili powder, curry for your meat, some masala for vegetables, or vanilla for dessert... make sure you don't forget to add them before the next step. Keep in mind that when cooked Sous Vide, the spices will not lose their flavor, so you might want to be careful with the stronger ones.

Step 4: Pack the Ingredients

Place the seasoned ingredients into the food-grade vacuum sealing bag or a resealable freezer bag. Spread the ingredients evenly. Add some butter or oil, if required, and seal the bags.

Step 5: Set and Go

Set the required time and temperature at the cooker or circulator. Once the water comes up to temperature, add the sealed bags to the water. Make sure that they are evenly drowned in the water during the whole cooking process.

What are the Advantages of Sous Vide?

Frankly speaking, the idea of food being cooked by itself without a loss of texture and at no risk of overheating is so attractive that Sous Vide doesn't really need any more reasons to become one's favorite way of cooking. Steaks, chops, chicken breasts, seafood, vegetables, and even large cuts of meat like lamb legs and pork shoulders can be cooked perfectly. There is no more need to poke the food with a thermometer, cut and peek at pieces, or jab it with your fingers.

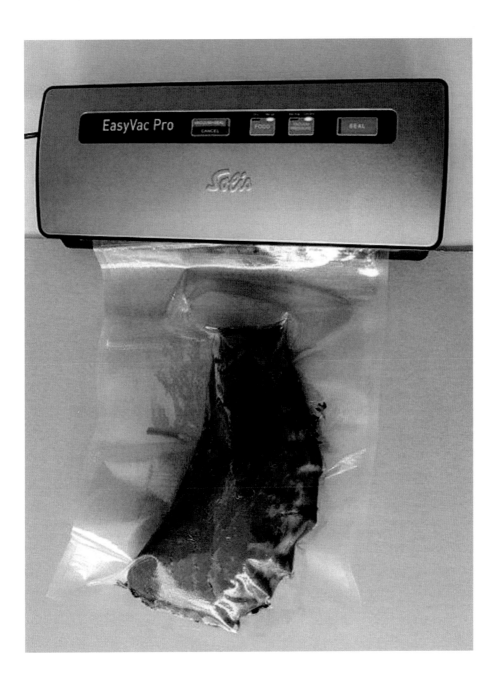

However, there are more advantages than that:

- So, the sealed container maintains all the flavor, juice, and useful ingredients that are otherwise lost or gone into the water.

- Meanwhile, the sealed container will **keep the food fresh for longer**, and will both protect your family from food poisoning and make sure that all the deliciousness of your meal is saved even if you don't eat it right away.

If we had to make a list of Sous Vide advantages those would be:

- Ideal doneness

- Great texture

- Strong and bright flavor

- No overheating or raw food—less risk for your health

- Minimal human involvement, so more time for yourself

- A fresh meal whenever you need one

Some Sous Vide Tips

Of course, when you are new to a cooking method, there is always a risk of messing it up. Here are some tips that will help you at each step of the cooking.

Tips for slicing and seasoning

- When slicing the ingredients, make sure that those of the same type are cut in **similar-sized pieces**. As all the ingredients are cooked at the same temperature and at the same time, they might not be cooked evenly if the sizes differ too much.

- **Don't use too much brine or sauce** or any other seasoning that will add much liquid to the bag. Otherwise, this extra liquid may interfere with the cooking process and mess it up.

Tips for packaging

- When placing food into a plastic bag, make sure that it is placed in **one layer of the same thickness.** This will ensure that the food is cooked evenly.

- When distributing food into the bags, remember that it's better to have **less than more**. Try not to place more than one portion of a meal into one bag. First of all, decent amounts of a meal will provide for even better evenness and texture, but also, once you've unsealed a bag, you need to have it eaten (no vacuum will be protecting its freshness and taste any longer).

Tips for sealing

- If you've got a vacuum sealer, make sure that you carefully follow all the manufacturer's instructions, but it's also a good idea to set two or three parallel seals—each above another—to make sure that the **bag doesn't let any water** in if one of the seals fails.

- If you are using resealable freezer bags, **press out the air** (as much as you can) and then seal the bag almost all the way. Initially, do leave a tiny gap. Then hold the bag by the upper corner and start slowly putting it into the water. When the water has come right up to the seal level, close the gap. The water will have done your job and pressed out the air leftovers.

Tips for cooking

One of the issues with Sous Vide is that the bag has to be drowned into the water throughout the entire cooking time. Here is some advice to help you do that:

- If you are using freezer bags, you can **clip them to the edge of the pot** or tub with clothespins or binder clips. This way, they will stay in the water, and this provides one more way to protect them from getting unsealed.

- Even sealed bags tend to float up when the water is circulating. To make sure that they are **correctly drowning**, you can put a pen into a binder clip and fix it at the bottom of the bag. The weight of the clip and the pen will keep the bag down.

- If you are cooking several bags in a relatively large tub, the idea with clips and pens may be a bit tiresome. In this case, experts advise adding some **ping pong balls into the water**. Light balls will cover the surface and won't let the bags emerge.

A Short Sear After

Foods cooked Sous Vide may look greyish and not really mouthwatering. To give it a nicer caramelized look, after sous vide, preheat a skillet and **quickly sear the foods**. This is also an excellent time to add some liquid sauce (if required), and check if any more seasoning is needed.

Eggs and Dairy

Crispy Bacon and Eggs

Servings: 2 | Temperature: 143 °F

Prep time: 10 minutes

Sous Vide time: 1 hour

NUTRITIONAL INFO (PER SERVING):

Calories 211, Total Fat 17g, Saturated Fat 5.9g, Cholesterol 440mg, Sodium 455mg, Total Carbohydrate 1.5g, Dietary Fiber 0 g, Total Sugars 0.2g, Protein 12.4g, Calcium 46mg, Iron 1mg, Potassium 144mg

INGREDIENTS:

❖ 4 large egg yolks

❖ 2 slices bacon rashers, sliced into ½" x 3" pieces

INSTRUCTIONS:

1. Prepare your Sous Vide water bath by dipping your immersion cooker and raising the temperature to 143 °F.

2. Gently place each of your egg yolks in the re-sealable bag, and seal it up using the immersion method.

3. Submerge it underwater and let it cook for about 1 hour.

4. In the meantime, fry your bacon slices until they are crisp.

5. Drain them on a kitchen towel.

6. Once the eggs are done, serve by carefully removing the yolks from the bag and place them on top of your toast.

7. Serve and enjoy!

Crème Brulee

Servings: 6 | Prep time: 5 minutes

Sous Vide time: 1 hour

Temperature: 176 °F

INSTRUCTIONS:

1. Heat the Sous Vide machine to 176 ºF.

2. Combine egg yolks, vanilla bean seeds, sugar, and heavy cream.

3. Strain the egg mixture to get rid of any bubbles present.

4. Add the mixture to 4-oz mason jars.

5. Rest for about 25 minutes to pop most bubbles.

6. Put a lid and also a ring on the jar and then tighten it.

7. Immerse it into the Sous Vide machine and cook.

8. After 1 hour, remove from the water bath and put on the counter to cool.

9. Put the jars in a water bath with ice to cool them completely.

10. Refrigerate for 20 minutes and then serve.

INGREDIENTS:

❖ 16 ounces heavy cream

❖ ½ vanilla bean, split

❖ ½ cup sugar

❖ 3 egg yolks

❖ 4 tablespoons granulated sugar

Optional Garnish

❖ 1 cup fresh

raspberries/strawberry/currant

NUTRITIONAL INFO (PER SERVING):

Calories 669, Total Fat 30.7g, Saturated Fat 18.4g, Cholesterol 210mg, Sodium 37mg, Total Carbohydrate 30.8g, Dietary Fiber 1.3g, Total Sugars 26.6g, Protein 3.4g, Calcium 70mg, Iron 0mg, Potassium 97mg

Egg Devils for Any Meal

Serving: 4 | Temperature: 170 °F

Prep time: 15 minutes

Sous Vide time: 1 hour

INGREDIENTS:

- ❖ 8 large eggs
- ❖ 3 tablespoons mayonnaise
- ❖ 1 tablespoon Dijon mustard
- ❖ Pinch of sugar
- ❖ Kosher salt as needed
- ❖ Ground red pepper as needed

NUTRITIONAL INFO (PER SERVING):

Calories 173, Total Fat 12.6g, Saturated Fat 3.3g, Cholesterol 330mg, Sodium 393mg, Total Carbohydrate 3.9g, Dietary Fiber 0.2g, Total Sugars 1.7g, Protein 11.4g, Calcium 51mg, Iron 2mg, Potassium 126mg

INSTRUCTIONS:

1. Prepare your Sous Vide water bath by dipping your immersion cooker and raising the temperature to 170 °F.

2. Carefully use a slotted spoon and submerge the eggs. underwater.

3. Let them cook for 1 hour.

4. Once the timer is off, use the slotted spoon to transfer the eggs to an ice-water bath.

5. Let them chill for about 20 minutes.

6. Peel the eggs and cut them in half lengthwise.

7. Carefully remove the yolks and mash them with the Dijon, mayonnaise, and sugar.

8. Season with some pepper and salt

9. Spoon the mixture into the halves and serve!

Sous Vide Yogurt

Serving: 6 | Temperature: 176 °F

Prep time: 30 minutes

Sous Vide time: 5 hours

INSTRUCTIONS:

1. Heat your Sous Vide to 110 °F.

2. Heat half and half to 180 °F in a pot, and then let it cool to about 120 °F. Add in yogurt and whisk.

3. Add the mixture to the mason jars and tighten. Put them in the water bath and cook for 5 hours.

4. Remove and put in the fridge; when chilled, serve, and enjoy.

INGREDIENTS:

❖ ½ cup plain yogurt

❖ 4 cups half and half

Optional Garnish

❖ 1 cup fresh
raspberries/strawberry/currant

❖ Berry syrup

NUTRITIONAL INFO (PER SERVING):

Calories 224, Total Fat 18.8g, Saturated Fat 11.8g, Cholesterol 61mg, Sodium 80mg, Total Carbohydrate 8.4, Dietary Fiber 0g, Total Sugars 1.7g, Protein 5.9g, Calcium 207mg, Iron 0mg, Potassium 258mg

Eggs Benedict

Servings: 4 | Prep time: 25 minutes | Sous Vide time: 1 hour | Temperature: 148 °F

INGREDIENTS:

- 10 ounces Canadian bacon
- 4 eggs
- 2 English muffins
- ½ cup fresh parsley, chopped
- 1/3 cup butter
- 4 tablespoons Hollandaise

- ½ onion
- 1 teaspoon water
- 1 teaspoon lemon juice
- 1 egg yolk
- ¼ teaspoon salt
- ¼ teaspoon cayenne

INSTRUCTIONS:

1. Preheat your water bath to 148 °F.

2. Add all the Hollandaise ingredients to a large Ziploc bag, and then place the bag in the water bath to remove air through water displacement. Seal the bag and place it in the water bath.

3. Add 4 eggs into the same water bath in another Ziploc bag (or direct).

4. Cook for an hour.

5. Sear the Canadian bacon until done, over medium heat.

6. Slice the 2 English muffins in half, and then toast them.

7. If need be, place the seared bacon and toasted muffins into an oven preheated to 250 °F to keep warm as you finish making the sauce.

8. Remove the hollandaise from the Ziploc bag once done cooking, and pour it into your blender. Blend until the mixture becomes smooth light yellow on medium speed; the mixture will be quite separated when you remove it from the water bath.

9. Crack the poached eggs with a spoon and do away with the excess egg whites (or place in a bowl).

10. Place each of the poached eggs onto a muffin slice and top with bacon.

11. Top generously with Hollandaise sauce and chopped parsley.

NUTRITIONAL INFO (PER SERVING):

Calories 675, Total Fat 51.1g, Saturated Fat 21.5g, Cholesterol 335mg, Sodium 2084mg, Total Carbohydrate 17.2g, Dietary Fiber 1.9g, Total Sugars 2.7g, Protein 35.7g, Calcium 105mg, Iron 4mg, Potassium 585mg

Poultry Recipes

Curry Chicken & Bacon Wraps

Servings: 6 | Temperature: 160 °F

Prep time: 10 minutes

Sous Vide time: 7 hours

INSTRUCTIONS:

1. Preheat your Sous Vide machine to 160 °F.

2. Season the chicken pieces with curry, salt, and pepper.

3. Wrap each piece in sliced bacon, sprinkling each with fresh lemon juice.

4. Carefully put the pieces into the vacuum bag.

5. Seal the bag, removing as much air as possible and set the cooking time for 7 hours.

6. Serve warm.

INGREDIENTS:

* 4 pounds bacon, sliced
* 6-pound chicken breasts, cut into 6 pieces
* 1 tablespoon unsalted butter
* 1 tablespoon ground curry
* 2 tablespoons lemon juice
* Salt and pepper to taste

NUTRITION INFO (PER SERVING):

Calories 2347, Total Fat 143.6g, Saturated Fat 42.8g, Cholesterol 725mg, Sodium 7309mg, Total Carbohydrate 5.1g, Dietary Fiber 0.4g, Total Sugars 0.1g, Protein 240.4g, Vitamin D 2mcg, Calcium 70mg, Iron 7mg, Potassium 3970mg

Honey Turkey & Bacon Wraps

Servings: 6 | Temperature: 160 °F

Prep time: 10 minutes

Sous Vide time: 7 hours

INGREDIENTS:

- ❖ 4 pounds bacon, sliced
- ❖ 8-pound turkey fillet, cut into 6 pieces
- ❖ 1 tablespoon unsalted butter
- ❖ 1 tablespoon ground paprika
- ❖ 2 tablespoons oregano
- ❖ 1 tablespoon liquid honey
- ❖ 2 tablespoons lemon juice
- ❖ Salt and pepper to taste

INSTRUCTIONS:

1. Preheat your Sous Vide machine to 160 °F.

2. Season the turkey slices with paprika, oregano, salt, and pepper.

3. Wrap each piece in sliced bacon, and then sprinkle with honey and fresh lemon juice.

4. Carefully put the wraps into the vacuum bag.

5. Seal the bag, removing as much air as possible, and set the cooking time for 7 hours.

6. Serve warm.

NUTRITION INFO (PER SERVING):

Calories 2247, Total Fat 134.7g, Saturated Fat 42.9g, Cholesterol 338mg, Sodium 7001mg, Total Carbohydrate 21g, Dietary Fiber 1.1g, Total Sugars 3.2g, Protein 227.3g, Calcium 60mg, Iron 5mg, Potassium 1769mg

Chicken Meatballs with Herbs and Tomato Sauce

Servings: 6 | Temperature: 142 °F

Prep time: 10 minutes

Sous Vide time: 2 hours

INGREDIENTS:

- ❖ 6 pounds ground chicken
- ❖ 1 tablespoon unsalted butter
- ❖ 2 tablespoons tomato sauce
- ❖ 3 tablespoons dried oregano
- ❖ 1 large egg
- ❖ Salt and pepper to taste

INSTRUCTIONS:

1. Preheat your Sous Vide machine to 142 °F.

2. In a big bowl, combine the ground chicken with egg, butter, salt, pepper, and oregano; mix well until even.

3. Form 6 meatballs.

4. Carefully put the balls into the vacuum bag and add the tomato sauce.

5. Seal the bag, removing as much air as possible, put it into the water bath, and set the cooking time for 2 hours.

6. Serve warm with white rice or mashed potatoes.

NUTRITION INFO (PER SERVING):

Calories 1186, Total Fat 47.8g, Saturated Fat 13.9g, Cholesterol 574mg, Sodium 573mg, Total Carbohydrate 1.8g, Dietary Fiber 1.1g, Total Sugars 0.4g, Protein 176.4g, Calcium 132mg, Iron 9mg, Potassium 1536mg

Turkey Curry Meatballs

Servings: 6 | Temperature: 142 °F

Prep time: 10 minutes

Sous Vide time: 2 hours

INGREDIENTS:

- ❖ 6 pounds ground turkey
- ❖ 1 tablespoon unsalted butter
- ❖ 2 tablespoons curry powder
- ❖ 1 large egg
- ❖ Salt and pepper to taste
- ❖ 1 sprig parsley, chopped

INSTRUCTIONS:

1. Preheat your Sous Vide machine to 142 °F.

2. In a big bowl, combine the ground turkey with egg, butter, salt, pepper, and curry powder; mix well until even.

3. Form 6 meatballs.

4. Carefully put the balls into the vacuum bag.

5. Seal the bag, removing as much air as possible, put it into the water bath, and set the cooking time for 2 hours.

6. Serve warm with white rice garnished with freshly chopped parsley.

NUTRITION INFO (PER SERVING):

Calories 1216, Total Fat 69.4g, Saturated Fat 12.6g, Cholesterol 653mg, Sodium 674mg, Total Carbohydrate 1.4g, Dietary Fiber 0.8g, Total Sugars 0.1g, Protein 166.9g, Calcium 169mg, Iron 13mg, Potassium 1687mg

Duck Leg Confit

Servings: 2 | Temperature: 167 °F

Prep time: 10 minutes + 10-12 hours

(refrigerate overnight)

Sous Vide time: 12 hours

INGREDIENTS:

- ❖ 2 duck legs
- ❖ 1 tablespoon dried thyme
- ❖ 2 large bay leaves, crushed
- ❖ 6 tablespoons duck fat
- ❖ Salt and pepper to taste
- ❖ ½ cup cranberry sauce for serving

INSTRUCTIONS:

1. Preheat your Sous Vide machine to 167 °F.

2. Mix the bay leaves with salt, pepper, and thyme, and season the duck legs with the mixture.

3. Refrigerate overnight.

4. In the morning, rinse the legs with cold water and carefully put them into the vacuum bag.

5. Add 4 tablespoons of duck fat, seal the bag removing as much air as possible, put it into the water bath, and set the cooking time for 12 hours.

6. Before serving, roast the legs in 2 remaining tablespoons of duck fat until crispy.

7. Serve with cranberry sauce.

NUTRITION INFO (PER SERVING):

Calories 495, Total Fat 43.2g, Saturated Fat 13.9g, Cholesterol 117mg, Sodium 373mg, Total Carbohydrate 5g, Dietary Fiber 2g, Total Sugars 0.5g, Protein 22.3g, Calcium 67mg, Iron 5mg, Potassium 57mg

Caramelized Chicken Teriyaki

Servings: 2 | Temperature: 140 °F

Prep time: 10 minutes

Sous Vide time: 1 hour 30 minutes

INGREDIENTS:

- ❖ 2 chicken fillets
- ❖ 1 tablespoon ginger juice
- ❖ 3 teaspoons sugar
- ❖ ½ teaspoon salt
- ❖ 2 tablespoons Japanese Sake
- ❖ 2 tablespoons unsweetened soy
   sauce

INSTRUCTIONS:

1. In a small bowl, mix the ginger juice with salt and 1 teaspoon of sugar.

2. Rub the chicken and leave it overnight to marinate.

3. In the morning, carefully put the chicken into the vacuum bag and preheat your Sous Vide machine to 140 °F.

4. Seal the bag, removing as much air as possible, put it into the water bath, and set the cooking time for 1 hour 30 minutes.

5. Mix 2 teaspoons of sugar with the sake and soy sauce, and boil in a small skillet or saucepan until the sauce thickens a bit.

6. Pour half of the sauce over the cooked chicken breasts and torch the glaze until it caramelizes.

7. Chop the fillets and serve over white rice, drizzling with the remaining half of the sauce.

NUTRITION INFO (PER SERVING):

Calories 308, Total Fat 10.5g, Saturated Fat 2.9g, Cholesterol 125mg, Sodium 1605mg, Total Carbohydrate 9.2g, Dietary Fiber 0.5g, Total Sugars 6.4g, Protein 41.8g

Simple Chicken Breasts

Servings: 2 | Temperature: 145 °F
Prep time: 10 minutes
Sous Vide time: 3 hours |

INSTRUCTIONS:

1. Preheat your Sous Vide machine to 145 °F.

2. Carefully put the chicken breasts into the vacuum bag. Add the butter, salt, pepper, and halved garlic cloves, and seal the bag removing as much air as possible.

3. Put it into the water bath and set the cooking time for 3 hours.

4. Serve with any sides and sauces of your choice. This is a really basic recipe, so practically anything will work amazingly!

INGREDIENTS:

❖ 2 chicken breast fillets

❖ 2 tablespoons unsalted butter

❖ Salt and pepper to taste

❖ 1 garlic clove, halved

NUTRITION INFO (PER SERVING):

Calories 382, Total Fat 22.4g, Saturated Fat 10.3g, Cholesterol 160mg, Sodium 208mg, Total Carbohydrate 0.5g, Dietary Fiber 0g, Total Sugars 0g, Protein 42.5g, Calcium 28mg, Iron 2mg, Potassium 365mg

Chicken Breasts with Lemon and French Herbs

Servings: 2 | Temperature: 145°F

Prep time: 10 minutes

Sous Vide time: 3 hours

INGREDIENTS:

- ❖ 2 chicken breast fillets
- ❖ 2 tablespoons lemon juice
- ❖ Salt and pepper to taste
- ❖ French herbs seasoning to taste
- ❖ 1 teaspoon olive oil
- ❖ 1 teaspoon butter

INSTRUCTIONS:

1. In a small saucepan, mix the olive oil with the lemon juice and the herbs and set aside for an hour to marinate.

2. Preheat your sous vide machine to 145°F.

3. Carefully put the chicken breasts into the vacuum bag and seal it, removing the air as much as possible.

4. Put it into the water bath and set the cooking time for 3 hours.

5. Heat 1 teaspoon of butter in a frying pan and sear the cooked fillets for about 1 minute on each side until golden.

NUTRITION INFO (PER SERVING):

Calories 175, Total Fat 13.4g, Saturated Fat 3.7g, Cholesterol 45mg, Sodium 708mg, Total Carbohydrate 1.2g, Dietary Fiber 2.1g, Total Sugars 0.3g, Protein 13.2g, Calcium 23mg, Iron 1mg, Potassium 23mg

Chicken Breast with Mushroom Sauce

Servings: 2 | Prep time: 10 minutes | Sous Vide time: 3 hours | Temperature: 145 °F

INGREDIENTS:

- ❖ 2 chicken breast fillets
- ❖ Salt and pepper to taste

For the sauce:

- ❖ 1 onion, sliced
- ❖ 2 garlic cloves, minced
- ❖ 1 tablespoon olive oil
- ❖ 1 tablespoon unsalted butter
- ❖ 1 cup button mushrooms, coarsely chopped

- ❖ 1 teaspoon olive oil

- ❖ 2 tablespoons white wine
- ❖ ½ cup chicken broth
- ❖ 1 cup cream
- ❖ Salt and pepper to taste

INSTRUCTIONS:

1. Preheat your Sous Vide machine to 145 °F.

2. Carefully put the chicken breasts into the vacuum bag. Add the olive oil, salt, pepper, and seal the bag, removing as much air as possible.

3. Put it into the water bath and set the cooking time for 3 hours.

4. While the chicken is cooking, make the sauce.

5. Heat butter in a medium skillet, and cook the chopped onion for about 2-3 minutes.

6. Add the minced garlic and cook for 2 more minutes.

7. Add the chopped mushrooms and cook on medium heat until the liquid evaporates.

8. Add the white wine and cook until the liquid almost evaporates; then add the chicken broth and cream.

9. Continue cooking until the sauce thickens, adding salt and pepper if needed. Set the sauce aside.

10. Remove the cooked chicken from the Sous Vide machine and roast it in a skillet on both sides until light brown. Add the sauce and wait just until it heats to the desired temperature.

11. Serve with mashed potatoes.

NUTRITION INFO (PER SERVING):

Calories 269, Total Fat 19.8g, Saturated Fat 9.2g, Cholesterol 58mg, Sodium 449mg, Total Carbohydrate 11.8g, Dietary Fiber 2.6g, Total Sugars 5.7g, Protein 10.7g, Calcium 64mg, Iron 2mg, Potassium 318mg

Turkey Breast

Servings: 2 | Temperature: 135 °F

Prep time: 10 minutes

Sous Vide time: 24 hours

INSTRUCTIONS:

1. Preheat your Sous Vide machine to 135 °F.

2. Put the breast in the Sous Vide bag.

3. Add oil and then add the poultry seasoning. Remove air from the bag and immerse it into the Sous Vide machine.

4. Let cook for 24 hours.

5. Remove the turkey and use paper towels to dry it.

6. Serve and enjoy.

INGREDIENTS:

- ❖ 1 split turkey breast, preseared
- ❖ 3 tablespoons poultry seasoning
- ❖ 2 tablespoons olive oil

NUTRITION INFO (PER SERVING):

Calories 199, Total Fat 11.2g, Saturated Fat 2.1g, Cholesterol 55mg, Sodium 401mg, Total Carbohydrate 1.8g, Dietary Fiber 0.3g, Total Sugars 0.1g, Protein 23.3g, Vitamin D 0mcg, Calcium 68mg, Iron 1mg, Potassium 19mg

Meat Recipes

Cider and Rosemary Pork with Caramel Sauce

Servings: 1 | Prep time: 25 minutes | Sous Vide time: 45 minutes | Temperature: 140 °F

INGREDIENTS:

- 1 pound bone-in, double-cut pork chop
- 1 sprig of chopped rosemary
- Kosher salt as needed
- Ground black pepper as needed
- 1 chopped garlic clove

- 1 cup of hard cider
- 1 tablespoon vegetable oil
- 1 tablespoon dark brown sugar
- Sautéed cabbage, if desired
- Sautéed apples, if desired

INSTRUCTIONS:

1. Prepare the Sous Vide water bath by submerging the cooker and increasing the temperature to 140°F.

2. Season the pork chop with salt and pepper.

3. Rub the chop with rosemary and garlic.

4. Take a heavy-duty re-sealable bag and add a ½ cup of the hard cider and the pork chop.

5. Seal it using the immersion method.

6. Submerge it under water and cook for 45 minutes.

7. Once ready, remove the bag and pat the chops dry using a kitchen towel.

8. Take a cast-iron skillet and add the vegetable oil; swirl it gently.

9. Add the chops to the skillet and sear until golden brown (approximately 45 seconds per side).

10. Allow it to rest for about 5 minutes.

11. Pour the sauce into the skillet from the bag, and add the remaining ½ cup of cider.

12. Add the brown sugar and keep stirring until it (the sugar) has melted.

13. Simmer for 1 minute and pour the sauce over the pork chop.

14. Serve with cabbage and apple.

NUTRITIONAL INFO (PER SERVING):

Calories 1865, Total Fat 127.3g, Saturated Fat 45.1g, Cholesterol 390mg, Sodium 1506mg, Total Carbohydrate 74.6g, Dietary Fiber 8g, Total Sugars 61.2g, Protein 103.9g, Calcium 207mg, Iron 7mg, Potassium 2254mg

Coconut Pork Ribs

Servings: 4 | Temperature: 134 °F

Prep time: 30 minutes

Sous Vide time: 8 hours

INGREDIENTS:

- ❖ 1/3 cup unsweetened coconut milk
- ❖ 2 tablespoons peanut butter
- ❖ 2 tablespoons soy sauce
- ❖ 2 tablespoons light brown sugar
- ❖ 2 tablespoons dry white wine
- ❖ 2-inch fresh lemongrass
- ❖ 1 tablespoon Sriracha
- ❖ 1-inch peeled fresh ginger
- ❖ 2 cloves garlic
- ❖ 2 teaspoons sesame oil
- ❖ 12 ounces country-style pork ribs

INSTRUCTIONS:

1. Prepare your Sous Vide water bath by adding the immersion circulator and increasing the temperature to 134 °F.

2. Add coconut milk, peanut butter, brown sugar, soy sauce, wine, lemongrass, Sriracha, ginger, garlic, and sesame oil to a blender; blend until smooth.

3. Add ribs to a Ziploc bag, along with the sauce, and seal using the immersion method.

4. Cook for 8 hours.

5. Remove the bag and remove the ribs from the bag; transfer to a plate.

6. Pour the bag contents into a large skillet and place it over medium-high heat; bring to a boil and lower heat to medium-low. Simmer for 10-15 minutes.

7. Add ribs to the sauce and turn well to coat it.

8. Simmer for 5 minutes.

NUTRITIONAL INFO (PER SERVING):

Calories 392, Total Fat 26.3g, Saturated Fat 10.8g, Cholesterol 88mg, Sodium 569mg, Total Carbohydrate 12.2g, Dietary Fiber 1.2g, Total Sugars 6.1g, Protein 25.9g, Calcium 48mg, Iron 3mg, Potassium 465mg

Lamb Shank Cooked in Red Wine

Servings: 4 | Temperature: 144 °F

Prep time: 10 minutes

Sous Vide time: 48 hours

INSTRUCTIONS:

1. Preheat the water bath to 144 °F.

2. Sprinkle the lamb shank with salt and pepper. Put it into the vacuum bag together with other ingredients and seal it.

3. Set the cooking timer for 48 hours.

4. Serve with mashed potatoes, pouring 3-4 tablespoons of cooking juices over before serving.

INGREDIENTS:

- ❖ 1 lamb shank
- ❖ 2 sprigs thyme
- ❖ 2 tablespoons olive oil
- ❖ ½ cup dry red wine
- ❖ Salt and pepper to taste

NUTRITION INFO (PER SERVING):

Calories 485, Total Fat 26g, Saturated Fat 8g, Cholesterol 114mg, Sodium 1372mg, Total Carbohydrate 19.9g, Dietary Fiber 4.1g, Total Sugars 6.2g, Protein 33g, Calcium 64mg, Iron 4mg, Potassium 32mg

Lamb Chops with Honey Mustard Sauce

Servings: 4 | Temperature: 145 °F

Prep time: 10 minutes

Sous Vide time: 3 hours 10 minutes

INGREDIENTS:

For the lamb

❖ 4 lamb chops

❖ 4 rosemary sprigs

❖ 4 tablespoons olive oil

❖ Salt and pepper to taste

For the sauce

❖ 4 tablespoons Dijon mustard

❖ 1 teaspoon liquid honey

❖ 1 tablespoon lemon juice

INSTRUCTIONS:

1. Preheat your Sous Vide machine to 145 °F.

2. Season the lamb chops with salt and pepper.

3. Put the lamb into the bag; add 2 tablespoons of olive oil, and 1 rosemary sprig on each chop.

4. Remove the air and cook for 3 hours.

5. When the time is up, preheat the remaining 2 tablespoons of olive oil in a cast-iron skillet, and sear the chops over high heat for about 30 seconds on each side until golden.

6. Whisk the mustard with the liquid honey and lemon juice, then pour the sauce over the chops and serve.

NUTRITION INFO (PER SERVING):

Calories 793, Total Fat 67.4g, Saturated Fat 24.4g, Cholesterol 160mg, Sodium 458mg, Total Carbohydrate 5.6g, Dietary Fiber 2.7g, Total Sugars 1.7g, Protein 39g, Calcium 113mg, Iron 5mg, Potassium 76mg

Lamb Shank with Wine Sauce and Rosemary

Servings: 4 | Temperature: 144 °F

Prep time: 10 minutes

Sous Vide time: 48 hours

INGREDIENTS:

- ❖ 1 lamb shank
- ❖ 2 sprigs rosemary
- ❖ 2 tablespoons olive oil
- ❖ ½ cup dry red wine
- ❖ Salt and pepper to taste

INSTRUCTIONS:

1. Preheat the water bath to 144 °F.

2. Sprinkle the lamb shank with salt and pepper. Put the lamb, rosemary, and olive oil into the vacuum bag and seal it.

3. Set the cooking timer for 48 hours.

4. When the time is up, carefully open the bag and pour the cooking juices into a pan.

5. Bring the sauces to a boil and remove the scums from the top of the liquid with a spoon.

6. Add the red wine and simmer until the liquid reduces.

7. Pour the sauce over the lamb and serve.

NUTRITION INFO (PER SERVING):

Calories 719, Total Fat 32g, Saturated Fat 10g, Cholesterol 306mg, Sodium 408mg, Total Carbohydrate 1.2g, Dietary Fiber 0.3g, Total Sugars 0.2g, Protein 95.6g, Calcium 53mg, Iron 8mg, Potassium 1181mg

Lamb Shoulder

Servings: 4 | Temperature: 180 °F

Prep time: 10 minutes

Sous Vide time: 8 hours

INSTRUCTIONS:

1. Preheat the water bath to 180 °F.

2. Season the lamb shoulder with salt and pepper.

3. Put the lamb into the vacuum bag, adding rosemary sprigs, olive oil, and garlic.

4. Seal the bag.

5. Set the cooking timer for 8 hours.

6. Serve with boiled potatoes, pouring the cooking juices over.

INGREDIENTS:

- ❖ 2 pounds lamb shoulder, bones removed
- ❖ 1 garlic clove
- ❖ 2 tablespoons olive oil
- ❖ 2 rosemary sprigs
- ❖ Salt and pepper to taste

NUTRITION INFO (PER SERVING):

Calories 484, Total Fat 23.7g, Saturated Fat 7g, Cholesterol 204mg, Sodium 320mg, Total Carbohydrate 0.5g, Dietary Fiber 0.2g, Total Sugars 0g, Protein 63.8g, Calcium 34mg, Iron 5mg, Potassium 769mg

Beef Burgers

Servings: 1 | Temperature: 137 °F

Prep time: 10 minutes

Sous Vide time: 1 hour

INGREDIENTS:

- ❖ ½ pound minced beef
- ❖ 2 buns for hamburgers
- ❖ 2 slices cheddar cheese
- ❖ 8 slices marinated cucumbers
- ❖ 2 tablespoons Dijon mustard
- ❖ 2 tablespoons ketchup
- ❖ Salt and pepper to taste

INSTRUCTIONS:

1. Preheat your Sous Vide machine to 137 °F.

2. Shape the minced beef into 2 patties, seasoning them with salt and pepper to taste.

3. Put them into a plastic bag, removing as much air as possible.

4. Seal it and set the cooking time for 1 hour.

5. While the patties are cooking, toast the buns.

6. Remove the patties from the bag, dry them, and roast on high heat for about 20-30 seconds on each side.

7. Assemble the burgers with cheddar slices, mustard, ketchup, and sliced marinated cucumbers; serve.

NUTRITION INFO (PER SERVING):

Calories 925, Total Fat 37 g, Saturated Fat 17.2 g, Cholesterol 261 mg, Sodium 1626 mg, Total Carbohydrate 54 g, Dietary Fiber 3.6 g, Total Sugars 15 g, Protein 91 g, Calcium 7 mg, Iron 510 mg, Potassium 1127 mg

Beef Tenderloin

Servings: 1 | Temperature: 133 °F

Prep time: 10 minutes

Sous Vide time: 2 hours 10 minutes

INGREDIENTS:

- ❖ 1 beef tenderloin
- ❖ 2 garlic cloves, minced
- ❖ ½ tablespoon dried rosemary
- ❖ ½ tablespoon dried thyme
- ❖ 1 tablespoon olive oil
- ❖ Salt and pepper to taste

INSTRUCTIONS:

1. Preheat your cooking machine to 133 °F.

2. Season the meat with salt and pepper to taste. Then grease it with the olive oil on both sides and add the herbs.

3. Carefully place the meat into the vacuum bag.

4. Seal the bag and set the cooking time for 2 hours.

5. Remove the meat from the bag and dry it, setting aside the oily herbs and garlic mixture from the bag.

6. Heat the olive oil in a skillet and roast the cooked piece of meat for about 1 minute on each side.

7. Serve hot, garnished with the reserved mixture.

NUTRITION INFO (PER SERVING):

Calories 315, Total Fat 22.2g, Saturated Fat 5.1g, Cholesterol 78mg, Sodium 634mg, Total Carbohydrate 4.2g, Dietary Fiber 1.5g, Total Sugars 0.1g, Protein 25.3g, Calcium 74mg, Iron 4mg, Potassium 361mg

Beef Stroganoff

Servings: 2 | Temperature: 136 °F

Prep time: 20 minutes

Sous Vide time: 1 hour 20 minutes

INGREDIENTS:

- 1½ pounds beef loin
- 6 tablespoons unsalted butter
- 1 cup button mushrooms, chopped
- 1 onion, finely chopped
- 3 tablespoons all-purpose flour
- 1 cup beef broth
- 2 tablespoons dry white wine
- 1 cup sour cream
- Rosemary sprigs

INSTRUCTIONS:

1. Preheat your Sous Vide machine to 136 °F.

2. Season the steaks with salt and pepper and place them in the vacuum bag, putting a piece of butter and rosemary sprigs on top of each steak.

3. Seal the bag and cook the steaks in the preheated water bath for 1 hour.

4. In the meantime, heat 2 tablespoons of butter in a skillet and sauté the chopped onion until translucent.

5. Add the mushrooms, salt, and pepper to taste, and cook until the liquid evaporates. Set aside.

6. Sear the steaks in 1 tablespoon of butter. Set aside.

7. Add 2 tablespoons of butter and flour to the pan, mix it well with a spoon, and then add the stock, wine, and cooked mushrooms.

8. Cook until the sauce thickens. Stir in the sour cream and serve the sauce with the chopped steak over mashed potatoes.

NUTRITION INFO (PER SERVING):

Calories 721, Total Fat 62.6g, Saturated Fat 38.4g, Cholesterol 157mg, Sodium 709mg, Total Carbohydrate 26.3g, Dietary Fiber 5.4g, Total Sugars 3.6g, Protein 15.4g, Calcium 273mg, Iron 5mg, Potassium 649mg

Beef Bourguignon

Servings: 4 | Temperature: 140 °F

Prep time: 20 minutes

Sous Vide time: 24 hours

INGREDIENTS:

- ❖ 1½ pounds beef chunks
- ❖ 2 tablespoons cornstarch
- ❖ 2 carrots, peeled and chopped
- ❖ 1 onion, peeled and sliced
- ❖ 2 garlic cloves, minced
- ❖ 1 cup water
- ❖ 1 tablespoon beef stock
- ❖ 1 tablespoon tomato paste
- ❖ 1 teaspoon dried thyme
- ❖ 1 bay leaf
- ❖ 4 tablespoons unsalted butter
- ❖ 1 cup button mushrooms, chopped
- ❖ 2 tablespoons flour
- ❖ 1 bottle dry red wine

INSTRUCTIONS:

1. Season the beef chunks with salt, pepper, and cornstarch, tossing it gently to make sure the chunks are evenly coated. Put the chunks in the vacuum bag.

2. In a large skillet, heat the olive oil and sear the chunks for about 3 minutes until lightly browned. Transfer the beef to the vacuum bag.

3. Add the carrot, garlic, and onion to the skillet. Then add salt to taste and cook for about 10 minutes, stirring occasionally. Add the vegetables to the vacuum bag.

4. Finally, add the bottle of wine, tomato paste, beef broth, and dried thyme to the bag, seal it, and cook for 24 hours in the water bath preheated to 140 °F.

5. Heat a large skillet, and combine 2 tablespoons of butter with the flour to form a paste.

6. Carefully open the bag and add the liquid to the paste, mixing well to avoid lumps. Simmer for about 5 minutes.

7. Add everything that is left in the bag, mix well with a spatula, and serve over mashed potatoes or cauliflower puree.

NUTRITION INFO (PER SERVING):

Calories 392, Total Fat 17.1g, Saturated Fat 9.3g, Cholesterol 107mg, Sodium 183mg, Total Carbohydrate 16.9g, Dietary Fiber 2.2g, Total Sugars 4g, Protein 27.9g, Calcium 46mg, Iron 18mg, Potassium 698mg

Lamb with Basil Chimichurri

Servings: 4 | Prep time: 10 minutes | Sous Vide time: 2 hours | Temperature: 133 °F

INGREDIENTS:

Lamb chops

- ❖ 12 ounces lamb, frenched
- ❖ Pepper
- ❖ Salt
- ❖ 2 cloves garlic, crushed

Basil chimichurri

- ❖ ¼ teaspoon pepper
- ❖ ¼ teaspoon salt
- ❖ 3 tablespoons red wine vinegar
- ❖ ½ tablespoon olive oil
- ❖ 1 teaspoon red chili flakes
- ❖ 2 cloves garlic, minced
- ❖ 1 onion, diced
- ❖ 1 cup fresh basil, finely chopped

INSTRUCTIONS:

1. Set the temperature on your Sous Vide appliance to 133 °F. Season the lamb with pepper and salt, then vacuum seal it together with the crushed garlic and cook for 2 hours.

2. Meanwhile, combine all basil chimichurri ingredients in a bowl and mix well. Season as desired, then cover and refrigerate to allow the flavors to blend together.

3. Remove the lamb chops from the vacuum-sealed bag after 2 hours of cooking, and then dry using a paper towel.

4. Sear with a scalding hot well-oiled pan, and then slice between the bones.

5. Top liberally with the basil chimichurri sauce. Enjoy!

NUTRITIONAL INFO (PER SERVING):

Calories 194, Total Fat 8.1g, Saturated Fat 2.5g, Cholesterol 77mg, Sodium 359mg, Total Carbohydrate 4g, Dietary Fiber 0.8g, Total Sugars 1.3g, Protein 24.6g, Calcium 36mg, Iron 2mg, Potassium 366mg

Seafood

Cheese Fish

Servings: 2 | Temperature: 135 °F

Prep time: 5 minutes

Sous Vide time: 20 minutes

INSTRUCTIONS:

1. Preheat the water bath to 135 °F.

2. Rub the fish fillets with salt and pepper, and then put the fish and olive oil into the vacuum bag.

3. Seal the bag and set the timer for 20 minutes.

4. Serve with the cheese sauce mix.

INGREDIENTS:

- ❖ 6 ounces salmon fillets
- ❖ 2 tablespoons olive oil
- ❖ Salt and pepper to taste
- ❖ ¼ cup cheese sauce mix

NUTRITIONAL INFO (PER SERVING):

Calories 287, Total Fat 21.6g, Saturated Fat 3.6g, Cholesterol 40mg, Sodium 638mg, Total Carbohydrate 7.5g, Dietary Fiber 0.1g, Total Sugars 1.3g, Protein 17.4g, Calcium 53mg, Iron 1mg, Potassium 381mg

Ginger Salmon

Servings: 2 | Temperature: 125 °F

Prep time: 1 hour

Sous Vide time: 30 minutes

INGREDIENTS:

- ❖ 8 ounces salmon fillets
- ❖ 2 tablespoons soy sauce
- ❖ 1 tablespoon liquid honey
- ❖ 1 tablespoon sesame oil
- ❖ 1 tablespoon ginger, minced
- ❖ Chili pepper to taste

INSTRUCTIONS:

1. Put all ingredients into the vacuum bag and set aside for 1 hour to marinate.

2. In the meantime, preheat the water bath to 125 °F.

3. Seal the bag and set the timer for 30 minutes.

4. When the time is up, you can serve salmon immediately, or sear it on both sides in a cast-iron skillet until it browns a bit and then serve over rice, pouring the juices from the bag over the rice.

NUTRITIONAL INFO (PER SERVING):

Calories 260, Total Fat 14g, Saturated Fat 2g, Cholesterol 50mg, Sodium 953mg, Total Carbohydrate 11.9g, Dietary Fiber 0.5g, Total Sugars 9g, Protein 23.3g, Calcium 47mg, Iron 1mg, Potassium 514mg

Salmon Teriyaki

Servings: 8 | Prep time: 30 minutes | Sous Vide time: 1 hour | Temperature: 104 °F

INGREDIENTS:

- ❖ 16 ounces salmon fillets
- ❖ 8 tablespoons Teriyaki sauce

INSTRUCTIONS:

1. Preheat your cooking machine to 104 °F.

2. Evenly cover the salmon fillets with the Teriyaki sauce, and then set aside for half an hour.

3. Place the fillets in the vacuum bag. Seal it, setting the timer for 1 hour.

4. Serve immediately with steamed white rice.

NUTRITIONAL INFO (PER SERVING):

Calories 91, Total Fat 3.5g, Saturated Fat 0.5g, Cholesterol 25mg, Sodium 715mg, Total Carbohydrate 2.8g, Dietary Fiber 0g, Total Sugars 2.5g, Protein 12.1g, Calcium 25mg, Iron 1mg, Potassium 258mg

Butter Shrimp

Servings: 4 | Prep time: 10 minutes | Sous Vide time: 25 minutes | Temperature: 125 °F

INGREDIENTS:

- ❖ 8 ounces shrimp, peeled and deveined
- ❖ 1 onion, minced

- ❖ 1 tablespoon unsalted butter, melted
- ❖ 2 teaspoons thyme
- ❖ 1 teaspoon lemon zest, grated

INSTRUCTIONS:

1. Preheat your cooking machine to 125 °F.

2. Put all ingredients in the vacuum bag. Seal the bag, put it into the water bath, and set the timer for 25 minutes. Serve immediately as an appetizer or tossed with penne pasta.

NUTRITIONAL INFO (PER SERVING):

Calories 106, Total Fat 3.9g, Saturated Fat 2.1g, Cholesterol 127mg, Sodium 160mg, Total Carbohydrate 3.9g, Dietary Fiber 0.8g, Total Sugars 1.2g, Protein 13.3g, Calcium 68mg, Iron 1mg, Potassium 143mg

Shrimp Penne

Servings: 4 | Temperature: 125 °F

Prep time: 10 minutes

Sous Vide time: 25 minutes

INGREDIENTS:

- ❖ 8 ounces shrimp, peeled and deveined
- ❖ 1 tablespoon lemon zest
- ❖ 3 tablespoons lemon juice
- ❖ Salt and pepper to taste
- ❖ 2 tablespoons butter
- ❖ 2 cups dry white wine
- ❖ Salt and pepper to taste
- ❖ Cooked penne pasta (4 servings)

INSTRUCTIONS:

1. Preheat your cooking machine to 125 °F.

2. Put the shrimp into the vacuum bag, and then add the butter, salt, and pepper.

3. Seal the bag, put it into the water bath, and set the timer for 25 minutes.

4. Carefully pour the cooked shrimp, along with all cooking liquid, into a medium pot.

5. Add the lemon juice, lemon zest, and 2 cups dry white wine to the pot.

6. Simmer the mixture until it thickens; pour the sauce over the cooked penne and serve.

NUTRITIONAL INFO (PER SERVING):

Calories 491, Total Fat 9.8g, Saturated Fat 4.5g, Cholesterol 228mg, Sodium 362mg, Total Carbohydrate 71.5g, Dietary Fiber 0.2g, Total Sugars 0.3g, Protein 27.6g, Calcium 75mg, Iron 5mg, Potassium 347mg

Seafood Mix with Tomato, Wine, and Parsley

Servings: 4 | Temperature: 140 °F

Prep time: 10 minutes

Sous Vide time: 2 hours

INSTRUCTIONS:

1. Preheat your cooking machine to 140 °F.

2. Sprinkle the thawed seafood mix with salt and pepper and put it into the vacuum bag, adding the tomatoes, bay leaf, dried oregano, garlic, olive oil, and white wine.

3. Seal the bag, put it into the water bath, and cook for 2 hours.

4. Serve over rice sprinkled with freshly chopped parsley and lemon juice.

INGREDIENTS:

❖ 2 pounds frozen seafood mix, thawed

❖ 1 cup diced tomatoes in own juice

❖ ½ cup dry white wine

❖ 1 bay leaf

❖ 1 teaspoon dried oregano

❖ 2 garlic cloves, minced

❖ 2 tablespoons olive oil

❖ Salt and pepper to taste

❖ Lemon juice for sprinkling

❖ Chopped parsley for garnish

NUTRITIONAL INFO (PER SERVING):

Calories 153, Total Fat 7.8g, Saturated Fat 1.7g, Cholesterol 58mg, Sodium 332mg, Total Carbohydrate 5.5g, Dietary Fiber 1.1g, Total Sugars 1.8g, Protein 8.8g, Calcium 56mg, Iron 3mg, Potassium 192mg

Butter Scallops

Servings: 4 | Temperature: 125 °F

Prep time: 10 minutes

Sous Vide time: 30 minutes

INSTRUCTIONS:

1. Preheat your cooking machine to 125 °F.

2. Remove the muscles from the scallops; sprinkle with salt and pepper.

3. Put the scallops into the vacuum bag, and add the olive oil.

4. Seal the bag, put it into the water bath, and set the timer for 30 minutes.

5. When the scallops are ready, dry them with a paper towel and sear in butter until golden on both sides.

6. Serve with Hollandaise sauce.

INGREDIENTS:

- ❖ 14 ounces scallops
- ❖ Salt and pepper to taste
- ❖ 1 tablespoon olive oil
- ❖ 1 tablespoon butter
- ❖ ½ cup Hollandaise sauce

NUTRITIONAL INFO (PER SERVING):

Calories 151, Total Fat 7.3g, Saturated Fat 2.4g, Cholesterol 40mg, Sodium 383mg, Total Carbohydrate 3.8g, Dietary Fiber 0.1g, Total Sugars 0g, Protein 17g, Calcium 31mg, Iron 0mg, Potassium 330mg

Salmon with Hollandaise Sauce

Servings: 4 | Temperature: 140°F

Prep time: 5 minutes

Sous Vide time: 30 minutes

INSTRUCTIONS:

1. Prepare your salmon by rubbing it with salt.

2. Let it chill in your fridge for 30 minutes.

3. Prepare your water bath by heating it up to 140 °F.

4. Add the salmon to a re-sealable bag, and seal it well using the immersion method.

5. Cook for 30 minutes under water.

6. Remove the salmon and pat them dry.

7. Sear if needed, and serve with the Hollandaise sauce.

INGREDIENTS:

❖ 8 ounces salmon fillets

❖ Salt as needed

❖ 1 cup Hollandaise Sauce

NUTRITIONAL INFO (PER SERVING):

Calories 91, Total Fat 3.9 g, Saturated Fat 0.6 g, Cholesterol 25 mg, Sodium 136 mg, Total Carbohydrate 2.7 g, Dietary Fiber 0.1 g, Total Sugars 0g, Protein 11.6 g, Vitamin D 0 mcg, Calcium 31 mg, Iron 0 mg, Potassium 234 mg

Vegetables and Grains

Cream of Corn Soup

Servings: 4 | Temperature: 183 °F

Prep time: 10 minutes

Sous Vide time: 25 minutes

INGREDIENTS:

- ❖ Kernels of 4 ears of corn
- ❖ 6 cups water
- ❖ 1 cup heavy cream
- ❖ 1 tablespoon olive oil
- ❖ Salt and pepper to taste

INGREDIENTS:

1. Set your cooking device to 183 °F.

2. Place the corn kernels, water, salt, pepper, and olive oil into a plastic bag and seal it, removing the air.

3. Set the cooking time for 25 minutes.

4. Transfer the cooked kernels with the liquid to a pot. Add the cream and water (if needed) and simmer on medium heat for about 10 minutes.

5. Blend the soup with an immersion blender, and salt and pepper to taste; serve with chopped parsley.

NUTRITIONAL INFO (PER SERVING):

Calories 266, Total Fat 16.4g, Saturated Fat 7.7g, Cholesterol 41mg, Sodium 192mg, Total Carbohydrate 29.9g, Dietary Fiber 4.2g, Total Sugars 5g, Protein 5.6g, Calcium 31mg, Iron 4mg, Potassium 444mg

Cinnamon Raisin Oatmeal

Servings: 4 | Temperature: 183 °F

Prep time: 5 minutes

Sous Vide Time: 40 minutes

INGREDIENTS:

- ❖ ½ cup steel cut oats
- ❖ ¼ teaspoon ground cinnamon
- ❖ 1½ cups water
- ❖ 2 tablespoons raisins
- ❖ ¼ teaspoon salt
- ❖ ¼ cup almond slivers
- ❖ ¼ cup maple syrup, optional

INSTRUCTIONS:

1. Preheat the Sous Vide water bath to 183 °F.

2. In a pint mason jar, mix cinnamon, water, salt, raisins, and steel-cut oats, and tighten the lid.

3. Shake the jar and immerse it in the water bath, and cook for 40 minutes.

4. Use a spoon to transfer the oatmeal into a bowl. If desired, sprinkle with maple syrup and almond slivers.

NUTRITIONAL INFO (PER SERVING):

Calories 142, Total Fat 1.4g, Saturated Fat 0.3g, Cholesterol 0mg, Sodium 160mg, Total Carbohydrate 29.8g, Dietary Fiber 2.3g, Total Sugars 14.4g, Protein 3.5g, Calcium 37mg, Iron 1mg, Potassium 162 mg

Butter Carrots

Servings: 4 | Temperature: 185 °F

Prep time: 10 minutes

Sous Vide time: 1 hour

INSTRUCTIONS:

1. Preheat your Sous Vide machine to 185 °F.

2. Place all ingredients in the vacuum bag.

3. Seal the bag, put it into the water bath, and set the timer for 1 hour.

4. When the time is up, serve immediately as a side dish or a starter.

INGREDIENTS:

- 1 pound small carrots, peeled
- 2 tablespoons butter
- Salt and pepper to taste
- 1 tablespoon brown sugar

NUTRITIONAL INFO (PER SERVING):

Calories 106, Total Fat 5.8g, Saturated Fat 3.7g, Cholesterol 15mg, Sodium 267mg, Total Carbohydrate 13.4g, Dietary Fiber 2.8g, Total Sugars 7.8g, Protein 1g, Calcium 41mg, Iron 0mg, Potassium 369mg

Potato & Curry Soup

Servings: 4 | Temperature: 183 °F

Prep time: 10 minutes

Sous Vide time: 50 minutes

INGREDIENTS:

❖ 1 onion, chopped

❖ 2 garlic cloves, minced

❖ 1 carrot, peeled and grated

❖ 1½ cups potatoes, peeled and cubed

❖ 2 cups vegetable stock

❖ Salt and pepper to taste

❖ 2 tablespoons curry powder

❖ Yogurt, chopped dill, and/or cilantro for serving, if desired

INSTRUCTIONS:

1. Preheat the cooking device to 183 °F.

2. Put the vegetables and curry powder into the vacuum bag, and seal it, removing the air.

3. Set the cooking time for 50 minutes.

4. Transfer the cooked vegetables to a pot, add the vegetable stock, and blend everything together using an immersion blender.

5. Bring the soup to a boil and simmer for 2-3 minutes.

6. Add salt and pepper to taste.

7. Serve with yogurt and chopped dill or cilantro, if desired.

NUTRITIONAL INFO (PER SERVING):

Calories 117, Total Fat 0.7g, Saturated Fat 0.1g, Cholesterol 0mg, Sodium 219mg, Total Carbohydrate 25.6g, Dietary Fiber 5g, Total Sugars 3.6g, Protein 3.5g, Calcium 46mg, Iron 2mg, Potassium 605mg

Farro Recipe

Servings: 4 | Temperature: 184 °F

Prep Time: 10 minutes

Sous Vide Time: 30 minutes

INSTRUCTIONS:

1. Preheat the Sous Vide water bath to 184 °F.

2. Mix farro, salt, and water in a mason jar and tighten the lid.

3. Cook for half an hour.

4. Spoon the farrow into a bowl and use a fork to lightly fluff.

5. If you want to enjoy it later, refrigerate it.

INGREDIENTS:

- ❖ ½ cup organic farro
- ❖ ½ cup warm water
- ❖ ¼ teaspoon salt

NUTRITIONAL INFO (PER SERVING):

Calories 200, Total Fat 1.5g, Saturated Fat 0g, Cholesterol 0mg, Sodium 148mg, Total Carbohydrate 37g, Dietary Fiber 7g, Total Sugars 0g, Protein 7g, Calcium 21mg, Iron 2mg, Potassium 0mg

Mixed Vegetables with Butter

Servings: 4 | Temperature: 185 °F

Prep time: 10 minutes

Sous Vide Time: 3 hours

INGREDIENTS:

- ❖ 2 large carrots, peeled and chopped
- ❖ 1 turnip, peeled and chopped
- ❖ 1 parsnip, peeled and chopped
- ❖ 1 medium onion, sliced
- ❖ 2 garlic cloves, minced
- ❖ 2 tablespoons olive oil
- ❖ 1 tablespoon dried rosemary
- ❖ 2 tablespoons unsalted butter
- ❖ Salt and pepper to taste

INSTRUCTIONS:

1. Preheat your Sous Vide machine to 185 °F.

2. In a big bowl, mix all the chopped vegetables.

3. Divide the vegetables into equal parts, and put them into vacuum bags; add the olive oil, salt, and pepper to taste.

4. Put them into the water bath and set the timer for 3 hours.

5. When the time is up, brown the cooked vegetables in a cast-iron skillet on the high heat with the unsalted butter just until golden.

6. Add the garlic and rosemary, mix well with a spoon, and cover the skillet with a lid for a couple of minutes.

7. Serve as a side dish or a separate vegetarian meal.

NUTRITIONAL INFO (PER SERVING):

Calories 161Total Fat 13g, Saturated Fat 4.7g, Cholesterol 15mg, Sodium 233mg, Total Carbohydrate 11.6g, Dietary Fiber 3.1g, Total Sugars 4.7g, Protein 1.2g, Calcium 47mg, Iron 1mg, Potassium 276mg

Sous Vide Eggplants

Servings: 4 | Temperature: 185°F

Prep time: 10 minutes

Sous Vide Time: 50 minutes

INSTRUCTIONS:

1. Preheat your Sous Vide machine to 185 °F.

2. Place all ingredients in the vacuum bag.

3. Seal the bag, put it into the water bath, and set the timer for 50 minutes.

4. When the time is up, brown the eggplants in a cast-iron skillet for a couple of minutes.

5. Serve immediately, sprinkled with sesame seeds.

INGREDIENTS:

❖ 1 pound eggplants, sliced

❖ 2 tablespoons sugar-free soy sauce

❖ 6 tablespoons sesame oil

❖ Salt and pepper to taste

❖ 1 tablespoon sesame seeds for serving

NUTRITIONAL INFO (PER SERVING):

Calories 226, Total Fat 21.7g, Saturated Fat 3.1g, Cholesterol 0mg, Sodium 601mg, Total Carbohydrate 7.9g, Dietary Fiber 4.4g, Total Sugars 3.6g, Protein 2g, Calcium 34mg, Iron 1mg, Potassium 289mg

Desserts

Vanilla Pudding

Servings: 6 | Prep time: 15 minutes | Sous Vide time: 45 minutes | Temperature: 80 °F

INGREDIENTS:

- 1 cup whole milk
- 1 cup heavy cream
- ½ cup ultrafine sugar
- 3 large eggs + 2 additional egg yolks

- 3 tablespoons cornstarch
- 1 tablespoon vanilla extract
- Pinch of kosher salt

INSTRUCTIONS:

1. Prepare the Sous Vide water bath, load the immersion cooker, and raise the temperature to 180 °F.

2. Take a blender, add the ingredients to it, and puree for 30 seconds until you have a frothy mix.

3. Transfer the mixture to a re-sealable bag and seal it up using the immersion method.

4. Submerge the bag underwater and cook for 45 minutes.

5. Shake the bag about halfway through to prevent the formation of clumps.

6. Once cooked, remove the bag and transfer it to the blender once more.

7. Puree again until smooth.

8. Transfer it to a bowl and allow it to chill.

9. Serve with a garnish of strawberries or your favorite topping.

NUTRITIONAL INFO (PER SERVING):

Calories 151, Total Fat 11.2g, Saturated Fat 6.2g, Cholesterol 124mg, Sodium 156mg, Total Carbohydrate 6.6g, Dietary Fiber 0g, Total Sugars 2.7g, Protein 4.9g, Calcium 73mg, Iron 1mg, Potassium 110mg

Banana Oatmeal

Servings: 4 | Temperature: 180 °F

Prep time: 5 minutes

Sous Vide time: 6-10 hours

INSTRUCTIONS:

1. Set up your Sous Vide immersion cooker to a temperature of 180 °F, and prepare your water bath.

2. Add all of the ingredients to a heavy-duty re-sealable zipper bag, and seal it up using the water immersion/displacement method.

3. Place it under the water bath, and let it cook overnight (or for about 6-10 hours).

4. Once done, pour the oatmeal into serving bowls and add your toppings.

INGREDIENTS:

* 2 cups rolled oats
* 3 cups coconut milk
* 3 cups skim milk
* 3 mashed bananas
* 1 teaspoon vanilla extract

NUTRITIONAL INFO (PER SERVING):

Calories 1131, Total Fat 45.9g, Saturated Fat 38.6g, Cholesterol 30mg, Sodium 750mg, Total Carbohydrate 124g, Dietary Fiber 10.4g, Total Sugars 83.4g, Protein 58.5g, Calcium 1855mg, Iron 5mg, Potassium 940mg

Vanilla Pears

Servings: 6 | Temperature: 185 °F
Prep time: 10 minutes
Sous Vide time: 20 minutes

INGREDIENTS:

* 3 ripe pears, peeled, halved and cored
* 1/5 cup water (a little more than 3 tablespoons)
* 1/5 cup sugar
* 1 vanilla pod, seeds removed
* 1 anise star

INSTRUCTIONS:

1. Set your cooking device to 185 °F.

2. In a small saucepan, combine the water and sugar, and then heat the mixture to dissolve the sugar and make the syrup.

3. Bring the syrup to a boil and then cool it down.

4. Carefully pour the syrup into the vacuum bag, add the pear halves, vanilla pod, and anise star, and cook in the preheated water bath for 20 minutes.

5. When the time is up, remove the vanilla pod and anise star and serve the pears.

NUTRITIONAL INFO (PER SERVING):

Calories 104, Total Fat 0.2g, Saturated Fat 0g, Cholesterol 0mg, Sodium 2mg, Total Carbohydrate 25.1g, Dietary Fiber 4.1g, Total Sugars 16.9g, Protein 1.2g, Calcium 43mg, Iron 2mg, Potassium 121mg

Black Pepper and Mint Pineapples

Servings: 4 | Temperature: 170°F

Prep time: 10 minutes

Sous Vide time: 1 hour

INSTRUCTIONS:

1. Peel the pineapple, and then slice it into quarters.

2. Muddle the salt, black peppercorns, mint leaves, and brown sugar with a pestle and mortar.

3. Use the sugar mixture to rub the pineapple wedges, and then place them in a Sous Vide bag.

4. Remove air from the bag, then place it in a water bath and cook at 170 °F for 1 hour.

INGREDIENTS:

- ❖ Handful of mint leaves
- ❖ Pinch of salt
- ❖ 1 teaspoon black peppercorns
- ❖ 1/3 cup brown sugar
- ❖ 1 pineapple

NUTRITIONAL INFO (PER SERVING):

Calories 70, Total Fat 0.1g, Saturated Fat 0g, Cholesterol 0mg, Sodium 153mg, Total Carbohydrate 18.1g, Dietary Fiber 1.1g, Total Sugars 15.8g, Protein 0.5g, Calcium 29mg, Iron 1mg, Potassium 94mg

Plums with Red Wine Granita

Servings: 4 | Temperature: 180 °F

Prep time: 10 minutes

Sous Vide time: 30-50 minutes

INSTRUCTIONS:

1. Slice the plums in half and remove the seeds.

2. In a saucepan, heat the sugar and red wine until the sugar is fully dissolved.

3. Place the plums along with the sugar mixture and the red wine in a Sous Vide bag. Remove air from the bag, seal it, then place it in the water bath and cook at 170 °F for 30-50 minutes.

4. Freeze the poaching liquid and serve the plums with the granita.

INGREDIENTS:

- ½ cup sugar
- 1 cup red wine
- 4 plums

NUTRITIONAL INFO (PER SERVING):

Calories 173, Total Fat 0.2g, Saturated Fat 0g, Cholesterol 0mg, Sodium 3mg, Total Carbohydrate 34.6g, Dietary Fiber 0.9g, Total Sugars 32.5g, Protein 0.5g, Calcium 5mg, Iron 0mg, Potassium 162mg

Sauces and Infusions

Infused Blackberry Syrup

Servings: 8 | Temperature: 135 °F

Prep time: 10 minutes

Sous Vide time: 2 hours

INSTRUCTIONS:

1. Preheat Sous Vide to 135 °F.

2. In a Sous Vide bag, combine all ingredients.

3. Seal the bag and submerge in a water bath.

4. Cook 2 hours.

5. Remove the bag from the cooker.

6. Place the bag in ice-cold water and cool for 30 minutes.

7. Strain the infusion into a glass jar.

8. Serve or store in a fridge.

INGREDIENTS:

❖ 1½ pounds blackberries

❖ 4 cups water

❖ 4 sprigs basil

NUTRITIONAL INFO (PER SERVING):

Calories 449, Total Fat 0.9g, Saturated Fat 0g, Cholesterol 0mg, Sodium 9mg, Total Carbohydrate 116.4g, Dietary Fiber 9.1g, Total Sugars 108.3g, Protein 2.4g, Calcium 61mg, Iron 1mg, Potassium 285mg

Honey Lemon Thyme Infusion

Servings: 4 | Temperature: 135°F

Prep time: 5 minutes

Sous Vide time: 1 hour 30 minutes

INGREDIENTS:

- ❖ 2 cups water
- ❖ 2 organic lemons, sliced
- ❖ 2 cups honey
- ❖ 2 bunches lemon thyme

INSTRUCTIONS:

1. Preheat Sous Vide cooker to 135 °F.

2. Combine all ingredients into the Sous Vide bag.

3. Seal the bag using the water immersion technique.

4. Cook the syrup 1½ hours.

5. Prepare an ice-cold water bath.

6. Remove the bag from the cooker and place it into the water bath.

7. Chill the syrup for 30 minutes.

8. Strain into a clean glass jar and serve.

NUTRITIONAL INFO (PER SERVING):

Calories 544, Total Fat 0.6g, Saturated Fat 0.2g, Cholesterol 0mg, Sodium 14mg, Total Carbohydrate 147.4g, Dietary Fiber 3.7g, Total Sugars 140.3g, Protein 1.5g, Calcium 138mg, Iron 8mg, Potassium 196mg

Cherry Manhattan

INGREDIENTS:

Bourbon infusion:

- ❖ 2 cups bourbon
- ❖ ¼ cup raw cacao nibs
- ❖ 1 cup dried cherries
- ❖ 4 ounces sweet vermouth
- ❖ Chocolate bitters, as desired

INSTRUCTIONS:

1. Preheat Sous Vide to 122 °F.

2. In a Sous Vide bag, combine bourbon, cacao nibs, and cherries.

3. Seal the bag, and cook for 1 hour.

4. Remove the bag from the water bath and let cool. Strain the content into a jar.

5. Fill 4 tall glasses with ice.

6. Add chocolate bitters (3 dashes per serving) and 1/8 of the infused bourbon.

7. Skewer the Sous Vide cherries and garnish.

NUTRITIONAL INFO (PER SERVING):

Calories 315, Total Fat 0.6g, Saturated Fat 0.3g, Cholesterol 0mg, Sodium 5mg, Total Carbohydrate 6.3g, Dietary Fiber 0.3g, Total Sugars 0g, Protein 0.2g, Calcium 3mg, Iron 0mg, Potassium 22mg

Blue Cheese Sauce

Servings: 4 | Temperature: 167°F

Prep time: 10 minutes

Sous Vide time: 20 minutes

INSTRUCTIONS:

1. Set your cooking device to 167 °F.

2. Carefully place the ingredients into the vacuum bag, seal the bag, and cook in the preheated water bath for 20 minutes.

3. When the time is up, pour the sauce into a bowl and blend with an immersion blender until even.

INGREDIENTS:

❖ 5 ounces blue cheese, crumbled

❖ 1/5 teaspoon sodium citrate

❖ 1/3 cup water

NUTRITIONAL INFO (PER SERVING):

Calories 125, Total Fat 10.2g, Saturated Fat 6.6g, Cholesterol 27mg, Sodium 495mg, Total Carbohydrate 0.9g, Dietary Fiber 0g, Total Sugars 0.2g, Protein 7.6g, Calcium 188mg, Iron 0mg, Potassium 91mg

Cranberry Sauce

INSTRUCTIONS:

1. Set your cooking device to 194 °F.

2. Carefully place the ingredients into the vacuum bag, seal the bag, and cook in the preheated water bath for 2 hours.

3. When the time is up, pour the sauce into a sauceboat and serve with lamb or beef.

Servings: 3 | Temperature: 194 °F
Prep time: 10 minutes
Cook Time: 2 hours

NUTRITIONAL INFO (PER SERVING):

Calories 50, Total Fat 0g, Saturated Fat 0g, Cholesterol 0mg, Sodium 0mg, Total Carbohydrate 11.3g, Dietary Fiber 1.3g, Total Sugars 9.3g, Protein 0g, Calcium 6mg, Iron 0mg, Potassium 62mg

INGREDIENTS:

❖ 1 cup fresh cranberries

❖ Zest of ½ orange

❖ 2 tablespoons white sugar

From the Author

Dear Friends,

I am glad to greet you on the pages of my cookbook **completely devoted to Sous Vide cooking**. Last year was very rich in events and meetings, but fortunately, my lifestyle has not changed, and I am still doing what I love most!

I enjoy spending a lot of time in the kitchen, **experimenting with new tastes, and verifying successful combinations**. And when choosing the meals, I most certainly keep true to my central principle: simple instructions and available ingredients. I am not writing exclusive recipes for master chefs—**I want *everyone* to enjoy them**!

This book is full of very different recipes! At first glance, they may even seem too different for the book-cover, but they all have one common feature—being vacuum-cooked at low temperatures.

Here I have collected my favorite and most successful recipes.
May you and your families enjoy these delicious tastes!

Our Recommendations

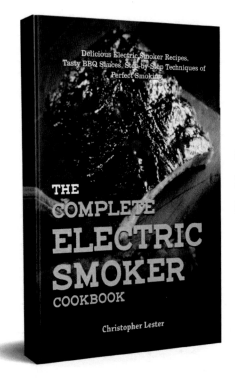

Complete Electric Smoker Cookbook: Delicious Electric Smoker Recipes, Tasty BBQ Sauces, Step-by-Step Techniques for Perfect Smoking

Dutch Oven Cookbook: Easy-to-Follow Delicious Recipes for One Pot Meals

Recipe Index

If you have a free minute, please leave your **review** of the book. Your feedback is essential for us, as well as for other readers.

Copyright

ALL ©COPYRIGHTS RESERVED 2019 by Christopher Lester

2
6618

Made in the USA
Monee, IL
26 November 2019